FAITH

A PART OF FAITH WALKER

BY

L. A. Crews

Edited by:
Jessica Peterson-Rogers

Day 1

I recall one day having to pay a bill. I was
wondering how I was going to pay it.   My rent
was due and so was this bill, my utility bill.
There have been times where I've had to struggle
and then somehow my concern was met. This
time just felt different because I had started
getting things together and I couldn't believe I
was back at this point. I had begun making
strides in my finances and couldn't believe I was
going back to the point where I had initially
began. It felt good to sleep at night and not
worry about how something was going to get
paid or how I was going to do for my girls what I
wanted to do and even what they needed done.

So many times it appears we forget that once
God says he is going to do something that he
actually does what He says. God is not like a
man or a woman. We don't have to worry or
wonder if He is going to do whatever He has said
He would do. The only thing we have to do is
trust and believe what was spoken is actually
going to happen.

Think back on a time when God said something
was going to happen and it didn't. In our society
today, we expect everything to be 'microwaved'.
Put a bag of popcorn in the microwave and it 2-3
minutes it's done. Things don't necessarily
happen like that with God. He doesn't rush to
do anything. After all, He took 7 days to create
this place we call Earth and it's a beautiful
creation. Don't rush what is coming. If you get

it too soon, you may mess it up and then you'll
have to start over again. Is that what you want?
I know I don't. Trust Him! He won't fail you.

Luke 12: 28-31
(28) "If then God so clothe the grass, which is to
day in the field, and tomorrow is cast into the
oven; how much more will he clothe you, O ye of
little faith? (29) And seek not ye what ye shall
eat, or what ye shall drink, neither be ye of
doubtful mind. (30) For all these things do the
nations of the world seek after: and your Father
knoweth that ye have need of these things. (31)
But rather seek ye the kingdom of God; and all
these things shall be added unto you"

What is it that you are waiting for God to
do? Write down one thing you asked God
to do and when it came to fruition. Now
write down what you are asking Him to do
now.

____
____
____
____
____
____
____
____

Day 2

I often wondered about the grain of a
mustard seed. I would often hear people
say have faith, faith the size of a mustard
seed. Growing up my grandmother would
cook mixed greens and which included
mustard greens. As I watched her clean
the greens, I saw how large a mustard
green leaf was. At any given point, the leaf
of a mustard green could span
approximately 8 inches. In my mind, that
meant the side had to be the size of an
orange seed. It wasn't until I became an
adult and saw the actual size of a mustard
seed. This seed is no bigger than the head
of a push pin yet it grows into something
more than 100 times its size. The seed is
planted in soil (your faith is in the infant
stage when you first begin your walk with
God) and as time goes on it begins to grow
because it rains and the nutrients in the
soil germinate the seed (as you read and
hear the Word, your faith grows).

What we need to grow naturally is similar
to what is needed spiritually. Naturally,
as babies we are on milk for nutrition and
once our systems begin to mature, we can
graduate to cereal then solid food when
our teeth come in. Looking at it
spiritually, as we get older, we should be
able to handle more than the scripture
'Jesus wept'. As we read our word daily
and hang around those of the same belief,

our faith grows affording us the ability to stand with assurance and holy boldness and not worry about what we are experiencing.

Lean on what you already know-God's ability to not fail or forget His promise. Seeds always grow and produce what they were desired to produce. Pressure squeezes out everything that it comes in contact with. If you are experiencing trials and problems, it helps not to look at the problem but look at what is being produced out of the problem. Your strength, your fortitude and your ability to overcome.

Matthew 17:20

"And Jesus said unto them, Because of your unbelief for verily I say unto you, If he have faith as a grain of mustard seed, ye shall say unto this mountain, Remove hence to yonder place; and it shall remove; and nothing shall be impossible unto you"

Recall your biggest problem you faced. How was it resolved? Did you survive? What helped you through that time?

____

____

____

____

____

____

Day 3

I have noticed in recent years there has been an escalation of suicides. People seem to have no hope or even at times belief that whatever they are going through won't improve. Don't get me wrong I fully understand if someone is terminally ill. Yet is there anything too hard for God? There are multiple reasons why people commit suicide. Some because of financial woes, other medical woes, among our young people it seems that bullying (both cyber and in person) are among the top excuses. Yet in all of this, the enemy uses these cracks, or what I call humanistic moments, to gain entry into our thought processes. Our society has become so impersonal that we as a people would rather text someone than call them. Nothing replaces the ability to hear a person's voice or even see their face.

I have had moments when I will pick up the phone and tell someone I needed to hear your voice, a text wouldn't do. It's in that moment, where we as a sister, friend, and confidant can actually discern if a person is doing well or not. There is a saying "a picture is worth a thousand words" (1) well, hearing a person's voice is invaluable.

Some of us feel that whatever we are going through can't and won't get better. Yes, money is a requirement in this world to survive, so is faith. People have lost their money, a house, vehicles and even employment but if you have faith; it will say 'yes I may have lost those things but I still have Jesus and me and with that team, I CAN WIN'. Faith says I can, when you feel like you can't. Faith says I will, when it looks like you won't. Faith says it will work out when you have been counted out. Allow yourself to become a faith walker and not a faithless runner. Fear cancels out faith. Faith will knock fear out of the park every time you use it. Faith is the home run of life's ballgame. Don't let fear strike you out.

Mark 4:40-41

"And he said unto them, Why are ye so fearful? How is it that ye have no faith? And they feared exceedingly, and said one to another, What manner of man is this, that even the wind and the sea obey him?"

What is your biggest fear? If you were to look at the positive side of this negative (fear) what would it be? Do you think you can practice the positive for 21 days? If so, what would that look like to practice it?

____

____

____

____

____

____

____

Day 4

Many people go through life with a hope in the people they are married to, work with and even spend large amounts of time with. It's okay to trust someone who, over time, has proven themselves trustworthy. However, my question to you, how do you have faith in someone who has the same capabilities and limitations as you? How does one believe in the human aspect of a person when that person doesn't know if something is going to work out or not?

Jeremiah 29:11 tells says "For I know the thoughts that I think toward you, saith the Lord, thoughts of peace, and not of evil, to give you an expected end". The Lord's thoughts are not ours nor are His ways of thinking our way. God doesn't have evil thoughts about anyone because He is love. Good and evil cannot occupy the same space simultaneously, therefore faith and doubt cannot coexist together. It is our hope that our lives will be exactly like we want it or even moreso like the dreams we have. We go through each day believing and speaking that better is coming, yet we often don't have the faith.

Jesus came to restore what was broken in the Garden of Eden and to tell us that God loves each one of us and to believe in Him. Having a belief in God is the first step in developing one's faith. In that faith, we know that even if it doesn't look good, it's going to turn out good, just for us.

God has never failed and is unable to fail. Whatever He says is going to happen trust and believe it will. Numbers 23:19 tells us "God is not a man that he should lie, neither the son of man, that he should repent; hath he said, and shall he not do it? Or hath he spoken, and shall he not make it good?" Often times we as humans have good intentions to do what we said we were going to do and either something may come up or we change our minds. God is not like us. He's going to do just what He said He would. Starting to have faith in God is as simple as 1-2-3.

Mark 11:22 is a simple verse "And Jesus answering saith unto them, Have faith in God".

Do you want to give one thing to God to see if you can start exercising your faith? If so, what is it and why?

____

____

____

____

____

____

____

Day 5

A farmer plants a seed expecting for that seed to grow into a plant, vegetable or fruit. For example, if you are a blueberry person as I am, then you can't wait until it is harvest time. Here's the process: when someone gets a blueberry plant they have to soak the roots of that plant for 3-6 hours. While those roots are soaking, you dig a hole for planting. Before you plant your blueberry bush, it is recommended to remove any damaged roots as these will not produce a healthy blueberry bush. When you plant your bush before covering the roots with dirt, organic matter has to be put into the hole as well for feeding purposes. Heavy watering is recommended the initial 2-3 weeks after planting.

After fertilizing, pruning and more watering, it typically takes approximately two years before the blueberry bush will prolifically produce what we end up with on our tables, dark blue blueberries. The final product takes time and that bush has to go through a process. The blueberry bush isn't planted one week and berries ready the next. For me, there is nothing worse than having fruit that isn't ripe. It is disgusting.

It's the same process for our faith. Faith doesn't just happen, it takes time for faith

to mature and withstand life situations.
Our faith begins when we begin our walk
with God. As we take our salvation work
day by day, the trials (organic matter) help
our faith to grow. The Holy Spirit is the
water we need for our faith to grow
because He reminds us how much God
loves us. Trust the process of your faith
growing and remember God is always with
you. As we go through life, faith helps us
realize that we are not going through
anything alone and everything IS GOING
TO BE ALRIGHT!!!

Luke 17:5
"And the apostles said unto the Lord,
Increase our faith"

How would you like to see your faith
increase? How hard do you feel it would be
to allow it to grow?

____

____

____

____

____

____

____

____

Day 6

Imagine you are driving on a mountain road and there is a rockslide. There is a large boulder sitting in the middle of the road and you are unable to pass. What if you were able to tell that boulder to break itself in small rocks so you would be able to pass and it would be out of the way? Faith is believing that you can do something even when it looks impossible to the naked eye. There have been many times I have had people tell me something I wanted to do didn't make sense. Naturally, it sounded insane yet I knew, spiritually it wasn't hard because of what I believed.

When we are going through life and a tough situation presents itself, it is easy to become discouraged. After all we are human beings and we can often times become discouraged. However in those times of discouragement, when we stand on the events of our past-and believe the thing we are facing can be overcome as well. Think about the toughest situation you may be facing at this very moment. Now if you think back on another situation where you thought you weren't going to make it but somehow some way things turned out okay. You see, it's in those difficult moments when we stand on our faith and watch everything unfold right before our own eyes and the eyes of bystanders.

I hear you saying, you just know understand, I've never been in the situation before and I'm not sure things will work out like they did before. Ask yourself this question, haven't I said that before? Haven't I felt or thought things weren't going to work out before in my life? Now please don't get me wrong, because there are times when things just don't work out like we want them to YET, they work out like they're supposed to. Psalm 37:25 says "I have been young, and now am old; Yet I have not seen the righteous forsaken, nor his descendants begging bread". So in other words, if we as the righteous (people conducting ourselves in an upright, honorable or commendable manner before God) believers continue to trust in Him, then He will do what He said in our lives. God is not going to go back on His word so continue to believe and have faith in His Word and watch your problems be resolved right before your very eyes.

Luke 17:6
"And the Lord said, If ye had faith as a grain of mustard see, ye might say unto this sycamore tree, Be thou plucked up by the root, and be though planted in the sea; and it should obey you"

What is your problem you are facing right now? Are you willing to let God solve it for you? Why or why not?

____

____

____

____

____

____

____

Day 7

In the area of the country where I live, we have all four seasons. Depending on the season we are in, it is a good possibility we can experience all four seasons in one day. The Midwest is truly not for the faint at heart when it comes to the weather. I recall in 2010-11 winter we experienced a severe snow storm where all major highways were closed, and a state of emergency was issued. Our main highway that runs north and south through my state was closed. I had to drive home through the storm. I had just worked my 8 hour shift at the police department where I was an officer and assigned to our dispatch center. As I drove home that night after midnight in my 4 door vehicle I named Cobbie (long O and not after the basketball player) I noticed quite a few vehicles that had stopped on the highway, including semi tractors. I could barely see yet I knew God was not going to allow anything to happen to me on that highway, why did I believe that? Thanks for asking, it's because I had a talk with God and I told him I was trusting Him to get me home to my children safely. As I continued driving I began to notice the roads were becoming slicker and more snow covered. I slipped and slid on that highway until I made it to the exit for the next highway that would take me a little further home. What was supposed to have taken me 15-20 minutes to get home took an hour. As I pulled into my driveway to my townhouse, there was so much snow I could not get to parking space. It was okay because I politely walked to my front door and went to bed. Notice I said I made it home. Faith says despite the obstacles I face, I will still make it. Faith says no matter what it costs me, I'm still going to overcome this issue. Faith says no matter what is going on around me, if I keep my eyes on what I'm supposed to do I'll be okay. When I looked around me driving home I became nervous because although I am an adult, I had not experienced a storm like that one. God tells us he will give us peace in the midst of the storm and it was that peace that reinforced the faith I was exercising during this storm. Keep your eyes on God and watch how you are guided through your storms.

Romans 5:1
"Therefore being justified by faith, we have peace with God through our Lord Jesus Christ"

Write down how you think you can begin to trust God.

____

____

____

____

Day 8

I recall one day while sitting in church and it was offering time. I had been tithing from my net which I thought was good seeing as crazy as it sounds I never really knew what my salary was because I didn't keep a budget (crazy right). It's okay I know I'm not the only one. Anyway, I was sitting and God spoke to me and said "start tithing from your gross". Mind you I'm sitting here getting ready to write my check for my tithes. Now let me just say I tithed off my net (what I brought home) however I would tithe from my tax return also so I thought I was doing pretty good. Nope, as pen was about to begin writing that specific amount He tells me this. Now I'm sitting here like a deer in headlights because I don't know what my gross is. I have a full conversation with Him like "I don't know what my gross is so is it okay I do it off my gross the next time I get paid". His exact words to me were "I'm going to trust you with this". Can you imagine hearing God tell you he's going to trust you with your word? Now you may lie to some people but God yeah I was not risking that at all. So now this meant I had to go home and look at my check stubs. I got home and saw what my gross was and my mouth hit the floor. I literally looked at my check stub and said "I have to give you 10% of this?" Then the first verse to come to my head (thanks Holy Spirit) was Matthew 22:21 "They say unto him, Caesar's, then saith he unto them, Render therefore unto Caesar the things which are Caesar's; and unto God the things that are God's".

This was going to require a whole different level of faith on my part because this meant I would have less money to work with for my household (natural thinking). Yet my obedience to giving 10% would mean my 90% would become more blessed and eventually multiply. So I had no choice other than to be obedient. I have to say even when I didn't think I would be able to do somethings God would always make a way. So my obedience in practicing my faith and trusting Him has outweighed the shock factor of me tithing off my gross.

Romans 1:5

"By whom we have received grace and apostleship, for obedience to the faith among all nations, for his name"

Think of a time you didn't think God would do what He said. What happened?

____

____

____

____

Day 9

I always wanted a black vehicle. I also
always wanted a new vehicle. In 2016
that opportunity presented itself. I
previously owned a Dodge Journey and
had paid that vehicle off and was happy I
didn't have a car note. I was content to
ride around in that SUV until the wheels
came off or I really had to purchase a new
vehicle. I had been enjoying the luxury of
not having a car note until one day I was
driving to a client's house and heard a
noise that sounded as if the wheels of my
vehicle were about to fall off. I
immediately turned around and drove
back to the office. I sat there in disbelief
and bewilderment because as a contractor
if I didn't see my clients I didn't earn
money. I then began to talk with some
coworkers about the sound I'd heard and
the possibility I may have to purchase a
new vehicle. Long story short I began
looking for new vehicles upon the
suggestion of a coworker and her delight
in the vehicle she owned. I went to one
dealership and they had that vehicle
however it didn't "speak to me" so I went
to another one immediately down the
street. As I looked at the vehicles on the
used car lot I heard the Holy Spirit say go
to the new car side. Again me, being me
asked "are you sure?" So I go and as a

salesperson comes out the Holy Spirit said this is who you will work with. It took only one hour for me to complete the sale of my new vehicle and drive off the lot with a brand new black SUV.

Not knowing how the process was going to go - and what to expect- I walked by faith listening to what God was telling me. If I had walked by my own sight I probably wouldn't have received such a great deal on a brand new vehicle and still enjoy the fruits of my obedience and faith in God. When we walk according to our spiritual sight and not natural sight amazing things happen in our lives. Faith allows us to have 20/20 vision because we listen to God's voice and not look with our own eyes.

2 Corinthians 5:7

"For we walk by faith and not by sight"

Think about what may be causing you to not listen to the voice of God so your faith can increase? Are you willing to sacrifice that thing? Why or why not?

____

____

____

____

____

____

Day 10

I have found myself thinking back on
some stories that my grandfather used to
tell me. He spoke of how he would walk
miles to go to school and then at a young
age stopped attending because in those
days it was more common for the boys to
quit school and begin working around the
age of 10. My grandfather told me when
he was old enough began working in a
mine. He worked there until the people
found out how old he really was and they
told him he wasn't allowed to work there
any longer. What did he decide to do? He
moved up north as a lot of people did back
in those days and began working multiple
jobs. He married my grandmother
brought her up north and they raised their
children. My grandfather stood on the
promise of God in that he was going to
have an inheritance for his children like
God promised Abraham. I recall my
grandfather going fishing and we would
have a fishing party in the basement of my
grandparents' home. My grandparents
were rich in love, wisdom and believing in
God. When my grandfather passed, I
really didn't know how I was going to
make it because he was my confidant and
my rock. What I learned was that his faith
in God taught me how to have faith in God
and to believe He would do the same thing

for me He had done for my grandfather. My grandfather was able to leave an inheritance to his surviving children just as Abraham did. He worked, saved and trusted God for the rest. He might not have had a high school diploma but he did have a doctorate in faith. Homer Williams Sr. made sure his light shone because his faith was so bright and strong. He would always tell me to just keep believing in God and let Him handle everything else. Well I can say, this faith journey has been just that a journey. Yes there have been highs and lows but what there has not been is a forsaking by God. Because we are all the seed of Abraham by faith, we are entitled to his inheritance. You just have to believe you are entitled to the inheritance and BELIEVE by faith you will receive it.

Romans 4:16

Therefore it is of faith, that it might be by grace, to the end the promise might be sure to all the seed; not to that only which is of the law, but to that also which is of the faith of Abraham, who is the father of us all.

How can you increase your faith?

Day 11

I have noticed the different ideas people in
the church have about how someone
should come to God. There are those who
expect a person who has no knowledge of
God to come dressed in their "best dressed
attire". Let me tell you, that's not going to
happen. More churches are becoming
more lenient with the dress code because
they understand the climate of our society
meaning how many people have no
knowledge or background about how great
God is. The only way they will learn is if
we as believers have patience and
understanding sandwiched between agape
love. I'm going to guess I had to be in the
2nd or 3rd grade when prayer was removed
from schools. It was then that the printed
logo on money "In God We Trust" was
truly tested. If we do not show people how
to trust God then how will they learn? In
the time we currently live in people expect
everything to be done in the amount of
time it takes for popcorn to be made in a
microwave. God doesn't work that way all
the time. He is able yet He doesn't always.
Jesus knew people came from different
backgrounds and cultures and he
understood how he had to teach them
about our Father in heaven. He knew if
he dealt with the heart of a person then
everything else would fall in line with what

He taught. It is totally unfair for us a believers and faith walkers to expect a person who is new in faith to have the same faith level and understanding about God and His Word as those of us who have been walking with Him for some time. If we love a person and show them how to love others, and how to trust in God, then eventually they will begin to exercise their faith and grow. The only difference between a new believer and a more seasoned believer should be the level of faith. Revelation 12:6 says "And they overcame him by the blood of the Lamb, and by the word of their testimony; and they loved not their lives unto the death". We have to tell others so they realize they are not alone in what they may be going through. Once their heart receives it then they can achieve a greater faith walk.

Acts 15:9 "And put not difference between us and them, purifying their hearts by faith".

What testimony do you have to help someone grow their faith?

____

____

____

____

____

____

Day 12

I have one biological sister. We are of the same blood line and lineage. We have similar features. We have a similar family history as well, same birth parents. Our dad was a pastor so yeah we are preacher's kids (i.e. PK). Our dad baptized both of us. Not many preachers have that privilege and honor from what I've been told. I say this to say just as we are biologically connected we are also spiritually connected. We are the seed of Larry and Gloria Crews and seed of Abraham. I recall when we were younger we had "faith" our parents were going to take care of us and we didn't have to worry about anything. Even when we had problems, and I know we did, we didn't think about if there was going to be food on the table or if our lights were going to be cut off because our parents, especially my dad, made sure we were good. I recall there were times he would go out to borrow money from family and he would do what he had to do in order to take care of his family. Well God does the same thing to those of us who are the seed of Abraham. He takes care of us. He will not allow anything happen to us that that won't benefit us and glorify Him. He has a plan for each and every one of us and it will come to pass. I will be honest- at

times it seems difficult to believe however
if you believe God is bigger and greater
than any issue you are facing then you
will accept the true fact that He will do for
you what He said he would. He told
Abraham he would make him the father of
a great nation because Abraham believed
him. Abraham believed God so much that
when this promise was made God changed
his name to show how much he was going
to do for him. Because Abraham was
about to have a great promise come to
him, God made his name more
extravagant to go with this extravagant
promise. Are you ready for your promise
from God made because you are a seed of
Abraham? I hope so because it's coming.
Keep believing and having faith. Let your
faith waiver not but let it be the ground
you stand on.

Galatians 3:7 "Know ye therefore that they
which are of faith, the same are the
children of Abraham"

Do you know who you are? Do you have
any doubts about your inheritance
through faith? If so, tell God what they
are.

____

____

____

____

Day 13

In the biblical days there was a debate
about whether or circumcision had to be
performed in order for someone to be
saved or not. Circumcision was a
requirement under the law yet when it
came to salvation many people wanted to
argue with the disciples about whether
circumcision was required. Let me help
you please because someone helped me;
spiritual and natural do not mix and
cannot operate together. One is going to
overtake the other and hopefully you will
allow the spiritual to overtake the natural.
This doesn't mean you won't feel anything
or your feelings won't get hurt. What I
mean is if we listen to our spirit man
closely then our flesh will not control our
thoughts. Learning how to control our
natural takes time and believe me when I
say, it can be a challenge yet this faith
walk is worth it.

I'd like to use my imagination and see the
faces of the apostles when this
conversation took place and them wanting
to ask the question, what circumcision
has to do with your salvation. Doing
something like that has nothing to do with
your soul or spirit man. Our boides will
be returned back to the dust from where

we came (Genesis 2:7) and our spirits will
return to our heavenly homes so what
whether or not a man is circumcised is not
going to determine if he gets into heaven.
Our faith in God through Jesus is what we
need to get into Heaven (Romans 10:9
"That if thou shalt confess with thy mouth
the Lord Jesus and shalt believe in thine
heart that God has raised him from the
dead, thou shall be saved"). Telling people
we want to see and live a better life
through faith shows that we care and love
them and we want the best for them. Tell
someone how your faith has helped you
through any problems or issues you or
your family have faced. We don't go
through things for ourselves yet for those
we are going to come in contact with.
Your strength has become stronger
because of your faith, not because of a
medical procedure.

Galatians 5:6 "For in Jesus Christ neither
circumcision availeth anything nor
uncircumcision; but faith which worketh
by love"

Write the names of people you believe God
has placed in your life to help them with
their faith and then tell them your faith
story.

____

____

____

____

____

____

____

____

Day 14

Sit back and remember your days as a child. If you were fortunate enough you were told to make a Christmas list. On this list, as children we wrote down what we wanted for the biggest holiday of the year. Some people were afforded the opportunity to go to the mall and sit on Santa Claus' lap and tell him what you wanted. He would sit patiently and listen to your list. He would then give a wink to your parent(s) and let them know he had the list and it was now their job to fulfill this list. We then waited with anticipation for Christmas to arrive and we would see what Santa brought us. We had faith that he was not going to let us down and produce if not everything on the list at least a majority of it. Some lists were profligate while others were modest. When Christmas arrived we ran to the tree to see what we actually had. There were times a substitute had to occur because the item wasn't available or our parents felt we did not need that item so they gave us what we needed.

As we have become adults it's the same thing. We go to God with an expectation from our wish list and He in turn does what he knows is best for us. We pray in faith believing what we asked for is going to come to fruition. There are those times when God will say no because we are not ready for them and if we get them at that time, we will mess it up. Just as we had faith in our biological parents we should have that same measure of faith if not more in our Heavenly father. He made us so he knows what is best for us and ultimately will do what is best for us. How much more will our Heavenly father do for us when we think about all He has done already. If God was the one who enabled and provided for our parents to do for us then don't you think he would continue to do the same for you as an adult? If you wait on Him to do what He said He was going to do, I promise he will BLOW YOUR MIND!!

Revelations 14:12 "Here is the patience of the saint; here are they that keep the commandments of God, and the faith of Jesus"

Take a moment and think when and how your faith become stagnant. What happened and why did you stop believing?

____

____

____

____

____

____

____

Day 15

Having daily concerns about what is going to happen and what we don't want to happen: is normal. We care about our lives and what takes place in them. What we should not do is worry about our lives. Some people consume their time with matters they have no control over and then wonder why their health is poor. Then, there are those who become obsessed with objects and material things where they lose sight of what they should actually be doing. We are told in Luke 28 chapter about how much God cares for us and to what extent He would go to show how much He cares for us. So if he cares for us why do we concern ourselves with worry? Once we say and conduct ourselves as children of God we have a secure future. We don't have to worry about how a bill is going to get paid; what is going on with our health; or even how our marriage is going to be repaired. If we totally cast our care on God we have the assurance he is going to fix everything because he cares for us.

Think like this. If you were to get into a boxing ring knowing the fight was fixed on your behalf, would you not still go? You would walk away with whatever the prize is, right? It's the same concept, we have the victory in every situation we have to believe we are victorious. So I would encourage you to walk with your head held high and remember there is nothing too hard for you and your God.

I John 5:4 "For whatsoever is born of God overcometh the world: and this is the victory that overcometh the world, even our faith.

Take a piece of paper and write down your concerns. Put a date on it and keep track of how much you worry about that matter once you have given it to God. Then write down the date he responds to those concerns.

____

____

____

____

____

____

____

____

Day 16

Let's make a cake. When we decide what type of cake we want to bake then we get the ingredients for this cake. We have cake flour, eggs, butter, baking powder, salt and any other ingredients to make this cake. We put everything on the counter next to the mixer and just leave it there. Is this cake going to mix and bake itself? More than likely not. It's going to take some work on our part. We have to preheat the oven and make sure we have the correct measurement otherwise the cake will not turn out like we like it. We believe we know how to make the cake and we also believe that the cake will turn out just as we desire, however if we do not put in the work there will be no cake.

Faith requires work otherwise nothing will happen. Think of the cake ingredients sitting on the counter and producing nothing. Once we begin mixing the ingredients we see our cake coming together. That's not it though. Once we have mixed all the ingredients then the batter has to go into the oven. We place the cake in the oven and let it start baking. The cake has to stay in the oven for at least 80 minutes. Just like our faith. Our faith requires exercise so it can become stronger. It has to be stretched in order for us to not fall apart when trials come around. If our faith doesn't become strong like a palm tree, then when a storm comes in our lives we will return to worry, doubt, losing sleep and possibly even returning back to the bad habits we used to participate in. Allow your faith to become stronger exercised and tested so you can become the best you God wants you to be.

Doing and believing what you do is for God's glory go hand in hand. We do with our faith so God gets the glory. We do with our faith so God is pleased because it's what he has told us to do. We do with our faith because we don't want to be stagnant in the kingdom of God.

James 2:24 "Ye see then how that by works a man is justified, and not by faith only"

What can you do so your faith can grow? How can you exercise your faith so it becomes stronger?

____

____

____

____

____

____

____

____

Day 17

Are you a Democrat or Republican? Are your wealthy or struggling day to day? Are you of a different ethnicity from your best friend? When someone who is not smelling the best comes and sits next to you do you get up and move? When you show partiality towards a person you are not operating in faith. Faith says we are all equal no matter our economic status, demographics, differences or similarities. We are to treat one another as we want to be treated.

In this matter, your faith would simply say' I am not better than him or her and they are not better than me so I'll treat them with respect'. Respect is a word many people do not understand nor fully appreciate. One definition of respect according to Webster dictionary, is placing in high regard or to have concern. Put yourself in the place of someone who doesn't have much and they have had a bad day already: now, imagine you coming and sitting next to that person yet you don't like how they look or smell and you move. Doesn't feel good right? Exactly, we teach our children the Golden Rule which basically says treat people the way you wanted to be treated, however somewhere between 5th grade and high school a lot of us have forgotten that concept yet when it comes to an expectation of others towards us we want the world to bow down. Having faith in God can also spill over to trusting others. Simply put, we see where people are in their lives and don't put more pressure on ourselves to expect more from that person until-they want more for themselves. If we allow our faith in God to manifest in the natural it can simply mean, we love people for their shortcomings and can encourage them to be the best they can.

God expects us to love one another because this is one of the main teachings Jesus gave us: to love one another as we love ourselves. Now the issue may be if you don't truly love yourself then you don't know how to love someone else. Have respect for someone by showing them how to have faith in God. Let your faith be a guiding light in someone else's life.

James 2:1 "My brethren, have not the faith of our Lord Jesus Christ, the Lord of glory, with respect of persons"

Write down a few ways you can respect others through your faith.

____

____

____

____

____

Day 18

There are 4,200 religions in the world. Of those, Christianity is the predominant belief that says Jesus is the Son of God who manifested himself in the form of mankind. Other beliefs make mention of Jesus however the recognition He receives is not that He is our Savior, Redeemer, Intercessor or our Lord. The Bible speaks of a time when people will turn their hearts away from God. It mentions that men's hearts will grow wax cold. We are fastly approaching those times. We as believers have to stand on what and who we believe in. There are some people who are willing to die and some do for the faith they believe in. We hear of suicide bombers overseas. We hear of individuals who use God's name to stand for different causes yet how many of us are willing to stand publicly for the God of Abraham, Israel and Jacob?

If we truly care what God says then our focus will not be centered on what man says. Our society has become inundated with seeking and trying to receive the approval of man. Once we stop comparing God to man, then our focus can truly be on the things that matter. We can begin to do the greater works that Jesus spoke about. We can put our attention on feeding the hungry, clothing the naked, housing the homeless and most of all, loving a person for who they are and not who we want them to be. It may be just me, however I have noticed a lot of believers (Christians) who are allowing too many things to happen. They complain in private about the issues yet Jesus says if we are ashamed of him before men he will be ashamed of us before God. I know one thing I don't want anyone of the Godhead to be ashamed of me. Therefore, my faith tells me to stand for what I believe and don't be ashamed of Him. I encourage you to not be swayed by others because everyone will not receive Him yet if you receive Him, keep trusting and believing.

2 Thessalonians 3:2 "And that we may be delivered from unreasonable and wicked men; for all men have not faith"

Is there anyone near you that doesn't have faith and believe? If so, have you witnessed to them? If not, why?

____
____
____
____
____
____
____
____
____

Day 19

Before I cut my hair, I went to a salon and had been going there for years. There were times that the salon owner would host special spa nights and at these events people could experience the different services she offered. One particular night as we were leaving God told me to pray for a woman that was there. I had never met this woman before and I can't recall if I ever saw her after that night. Anyway, after I prayed for her and began to pray for her son who I had never met I was told what was going on with her family and her son. I left that night not thinking anything else of that encounter. Here recently I was told after that night the son, who had been battling cancer, went into remission and had been in remission for some years. That in and of itself astounded me because who would think God could use little old me to do that. Nevertheless, the salon owner said it was after that prayer when the son had a miracle. I say this to say, God doesn't do anything by happen chance and it is not done remissly. I had to have had faith in the ability of God to do whatever needed to be done in that woman's life AND at that exact moment. Having a hope that something is going to be done is a small part of our faith. Not doubting it will happen is the largest.

God acts in our present to get us to our future not dwell in our past. Perfect example is when we ask God to forgive us for the sins we've committed by omission or commission he forgives us and does not bring those things back up to us. If we are constantly being reminded about our past it is because the enemy, Lucifer, is trying to keep you in a state of mind of guilt and regret. God tells us to move forward. Our past is our history. We can learn from it if we so choose however we cannot live in it if we say we have faith in God to do the mighty things He has promised us.

Hebrews 11:1

"Now faith is the substance of things hoped for, the evidence of things not seen"

Write down what you are wanting God to do. On paper or here write the date of the request and then when it comes to pass, write that date down. In between those dates, write what you did while God answered your prayer.

____

____

____

____

____

____

____

Day 20

Our faith can be perfected every day. How you ask? Just by doing what God says for us to do even when we don't know what to expect afterwards. We walk with our hands up asking for God to lead us in the right way. We ask him to order our steps and don't let us fall.   We walk with an expectation that something may go wrong yet we keep walking.

Our natural side can often be pessimistic. Our spiritual side is full of optimism and hope that everything is going to be okay. Look at Abraham when God told him to take Isaac onto the mountain and sacrifice him. Isaac had a justified question when he asked his father where was the animal they were going to sacrifice. Abraham's answer was short simple and full of faith "God will provide". Abraham had been told to move out of his country away from all he knew and loved because God made him a promise. So if God made him a promise that included his son, he knew something was going to happen he just wasn't sure.

As the owner of a vehicle, when my gas tank is low and even when the light comes on, I tell myself, I can make it and I will that vehicle to make that trip to the grocery store, run errands for my mother and even do other things for my children.

I will check the mileage and say "okay we're gonna make this until tomorrow when the direct deposit hits". My faith says I will not run out of gas stranded on the side of the road and my God says check your account. I asked God where did the money come from and he reminded me of a time I sowed a seed offering and said this is the harvest for that seed. My obedience to sow in according to my faith produced a harvest that wasn't expected to manifest any time soon. Just be obedient to the voice of God and watch how your faith becomes perfect.

James 2:22 "Seest thou how faith wrought with his works, and by words has faith made perfect?"

Start small (because a seed is small). Write down something you want God to grow using your faith. Keep a journal about this area and watch and monitor the progress.

____

____

____

____

____

____

____

____

Day 21

There have been a few times where I have opened my home to young ladies who needed housing. I didn't do it because I wanted recognition or attention. I did it because God told me to. God knew it would be a stretch for me because I am not that person that likes a lot of people in my home especially if I haven't raised you and I don't know your housekeeping habits or your mindset. Nevertheless, I came to the realization that what I was doing was planting seeds and not necessarily for myself however for my girls. I would just ask my Daddy God to honor my obedience and let the blessings from it fall upon them. Yes I have had the opportunity to reap from my obedience however, me doing what I was told to do made me feel good. Yes there were times I wanted to be disobedient and just say no you cannot live with me but I began looking at it as a teaching moment.

Doing kingdom work is a faith act. Especially when we take care of our brothers and sisters in the faith. If we look at it as mission work within our community it's make it a little easier to enjoy. Not knocking mission work in other countries because at some point we all may need help. What I'm saying is you truly get to see the joy on a person's face when they are blessed by something you did.

We can do all of these things while we are in good health in our minds, body and soul. It's somewhat difficult when you are sick or not feeling well to do anything, especially for someone else. If we put forth the effort while we are able bodies, think of the seeds you are planting for someone else to help others or even you when you can't help yourself. It may sound selfish, yet remember the golden rule we talked about earlier. A seed will only harvest that fruit which it planted out of itself. Try a simple act of kindness.

Galatians 6:10 "As we have therefore opportunity, let us do good unto all men, especially unto them who are of the household of faith".

What are some acts of kindness you can do within the next week? Write them down and then go do them.

____

____

____

____

____

____

____

____

____

Day 22

I recall a time I used social media and asked the question "I wonder what people will say about me when I die". What will their view be of me about my dash? What is the dash? The dash is the line between when we are born and when we die. Would my dash have meant anything? Would I have done what I was put on this earth to do and achieve? Has my life been ideal? I dare say no. Has it been enjoyable? Most of it. Have a had more difficulties than some? I would say yes but then that would not necessarily be the truth just because of many things I have endured that some have not. Life is not always easy. Even when we see people who are financially secure, they will tell you, the money doesn't make their life great, it just makes paying bills easier. It was never a promise from God that our lives would be easy, however He did promise that he would always be with us and wouldn't forget about us. I feel just knowing He wass with me, makes my problems just a little more bearable. Why you ask? Simple I give him my problems and I can sleep better at night. It's when I don't give him my problems and I try to solve them alone that I have sleepless nights, worried about how something is going to work out and what is to come next.

I would be lying if I said I have always had
the perfect faith because I have not. I
have tried to stay focused on Him so I
wouldn't worry and to prove to Him that I
do trust Him. Keeping my faith in God
has been telling myself, He cares and He
going to take care of it.

When you continue to trust God and let
Him do what He's known for doing- which
is not losing a fight; not forgetting about
us; him being true to his Word and Him
just being the I am that He is then our
faith- will continue to grow. Keep the faith
and don't waiver. There are no ifs ands or
buts about it! When your dash is closed
with that year people and God will say well
done my good and faithful servant, well
done.

2 Timothy 4:7 "I have fought the good
fight, I have finished the race, I have kept
the faith"

What legacy do you wish to leave behind
regarding your faith?

____

____

____

____

____

____

____

Day 23

Has there ever been a time when you had an encounter with a family member or friend and they needed something yet you didn't have what they needed? Or your friend or family member was experiencing something like an illness or something even more tragic and they were so distraught you wanted to take the pain away from them but couldn't? Did you feel helpless? Let me tell you, you are not the only one. At some point and time we all have or will come in contact with someone else who will need our support and we may not be able to give them what they need at that moment. We can do for others what we'd want them to do for us. If they cannot help financially or emotionally then we give them spiritual support. In order for that to happen we continue to commune with God outside of trials, issues and emergencies that way when a problem does arise, it's easy for us to go to him because the lines of communication have already been established and secured.

We give our faith to others, meaning when we pray for them, we attached our faith to theirs. We come in agreement with them about that problem that exists in their lives. I have said prayers where I tell God I extend my faith with theirs in order to let him know I am in agreement with them and believing Him to do what he said. God expects us to have a certain amount of faith and we are required to have some faith. We cannot be a good effective believer to the world if we don't have a certain measure of faith.

In the New Testament days Paul was steadfast in preaching about faith and teaching how to increase our faith. One of Paul's missions was to help believers understand what faith was and the importance of having faith. Faith is a main ingredient for a believer. Faith is necessary otherwise how can our testimony be validated. A faith not tried is a faith not proved. You need lungs to breathe so every day you try your lungs and every day they prove to be essential to your being.

Titus 1:1 "Paul, a bondservant of God and an apostle of Jesus Christ, according to the faith of God's elect and the acknowledgment of the truth which accords with godliness"

Write down an incident where your faith
was tried. How did you feel during and
after? Do you think your faith can grow
from this? Why?

____

____

____

____

____

____

____

____

____

Day 24

In preparation of writing this devotional I questioned God asking, are you sure you want me to write this devotional. At the ministry I had just joined not even 2 months prior we had a new members class and in that class we were to discover our spiritual gifts. Well, it was not surprise that one of my gifts is faith. I had been told this before by my biological and spiritual mothers. I had been told this also by a pastor. Yet taking the exam it revealed what everyone had been saying. So, I figured it was a confirmation to my question that I was supposed to write the book. The true confirmation in writing the book was when God gave me the scriptures he wanted highlighted and then it was the spiritual gift assessment.

There have been many things I have endured where I know it was simply my faith and my hope that God would do what He said. There are going to be some assignments God gives each and every one of us where the only thing we have to operate on is our faith. The enemy is going to come after each and every one of us hard because when he throws everything he has including the kitchen sink at us we know we are on the right track because he's trying to distract, discourage and deter us from what we are supposed to be doing.

Hearing that small voice tell you to call someone, to pray for someone, to go by their house or just send them a text is all we need to hear from
God. We operate in faith by obedience, meaning we do what we heard the voice tell us to do. We all have a purpose in life and it's up to us to find out what that purpose is. Our faith helps us to fulfill our reason for being. Faith is the fuel we need to activate our power source. Your life is not over, you have much more to do and your faith is going to help you get it done. Keep living, it's not over.

II Thessalonians 1:11 "Therefore we also pray always for you that our God would count you worth of this calling, and fulfill all the good pleasure of His goodness and the work of faith with power".

What do you think your purpose is? How can your faith help you fulfill your purpose?

____

____

____

____

____

____

Day 25

I recall in 2016 my mother became very ill.
My niece was at her house and I received a
phone call from her saying "grandma said
she wants you to come and pick me up so
I can spend the night with you". Long
story short I called the ambulance who
transported my mother to ER. After a few
hours in ER she was admitted and we
began a 2 week process of her being
placed in ICU, then IMCU then
rehabilitation. During this time, I was a
mental health contractor which meant if I
didn't see clients, I didn't get paid. My
sister came from Texas and we took turns
staying at the hospital making sure
everything that was supposed to be done
was. This included meeting with doctors,
nurses and specialists. The one thing I
knew I had to do was continue to hold on
to my faith because of how the doctors
were talking and what they said the
prognosis could be.

I recall one night I was talking to God
about her situation and telling him that he
knew I trusted him so my faith was there.
I then remember his answer to me which
was a question "do you trust me with her
life?" I was like you made her so yes.
Then I heard another voice saying "are you
sure you trust because other people's
mothers have had the same issue and it's
not been a good turnout". Immediately I

knew that voice was not that of my Daddy God and I told God if he healed her on this side or the other side I would still trust him. My mother was released and I stayed with her for a few weeks to make sure her medications were right and everything else that needed to be done for her was.

Yes it was difficult seeing a woman so vibrant, full of life and independent become the exact opposite. The one thing I knew was that I had to have faith in God that he was going to do what he told me and I kept believing. God isn't impressed by what we say, he is impressed by how we trust him with our very being. He wants us to have faith in him. When we press to have continued faith in Him he rewards us with the desires of our hearts.

Hebrews 11:6 "But without faith it is impossible to please Him, for he who comes to God must believe that He is, and that He is a rewarder of those who diligently seek Him".

Where do you find it hard to believe God? What area of your life do you believe you can fix and don't need God's help. Why?

____

____

____

____

____

Day 26

Inheritances are great. We don't always like the way we receive them however the benefits included in an inheritance are immeasurable and often times life changing. Inheritance as defined by Webster means something that may be passed on to another generation. Meaning it belonged to a person and they in turn wish to leave it for someone they care about or are interested in that person receiving.

Jesus did this when he died on the cross and rose from the dead. When he died we were able to receive the gift of faith. Faith is just one of the keys that he took back when he went to hell and freed all those who were across the gulf.

Isn't it great to know we have the right to so many gifts because of what Jesus did? Faith is one of those most precious gifts. Faith is the key that moves God and can move mountains. Faith is a precious commodity one that not everyone is privileged to experience its full capacity yet they can experience the benefits from it. With faith, believing for is different than believing in. We believe (for) our bodies to hold up for years. We believe (for) our children to have better lives than we have experienced. We believe (for) our lives to get better. If we can believe for these things, why is it hard for us to believe IN the one person who can do these things FOR us?

Don't doubt yourself and your ability to trust in someone greater than you. Don't doubt yourself in your ability to not worry because you think someone will say you don't care. It's just the opposite. You care enough to not allow yourself to mess it up for them or you.

Okay so maybe today was the day you allowed yourself faith to waiver. Tomorrow is a new day. The only person that will hold that against you is the enemy. Tell God you're sorry and let's do this again on tomorrow.

II Peter 1:1 "Simon Peter, a bondservant and apostle of Jesus Christ, to those who have obtained like precious faith with us by the righteousness of our God and Savior Jesus Christ".

Now that you know faith is an inheritance that only entitled persons receive, what will you do with yours?

____

____

____

____

____

Day 27

I am a mother, daughter, sister, friend,
minister, mental health therapist, social
worker and probably a few other
adjectives. I have multiple titles and
facets people are able to recognize me by
yet I am the same person. There are times
when I have to change hats as quickly as
one can blink their eyes yet I am still the
same person. My titles don't make me, I
make them. Your faith doesn't make you,
you make your faith. The more you use
your faith the stronger it becomes. Look
at faith as your muscle, the more you
work it the more it becomes what you
need it to be to carry you through life.

Your faith is a part of you just like we are
all a part of the body of Christ. In the
body of Christ we all have different
assignments. We all are responsible for
different entities that make the body of
Christ functional and operate as it is
supposed to. One person's faith may not
be as strong as another however we are
still apart of the body. We all love God
and want to do what He called and
appointed us to do. Unity- in this aspect-
simply means we work together, not try
and do the same thing. A lung wasn't
designed to work as the heart and the
heart wasn't designed to work as the
brain. Yet with all of these different
organs they all work together to make sure

our natural body works as it was designed. There are times when we try to do something we are not designed to do; chaos and discord arise causing misnomers and inconsistencies. When we don't exercise our faith, chaos happens in our life and we become misguided and often times begin making choices that are damaging to us and sometimes those around us. Faith requires a one on one line of communication between us and God. When the line of communication is strong, nothing can cause your faith to waiver. Be steadfast and unmovable in your one on one communing with God.

Ephesians 4:4-5 "There is one body and one Spirit, just as you were called in one hope of your calling; one Lord, one faith, one baptism"

What are some things that have interrupted your line of communication to interfere with your faith?

____

____

____

____

____

____

____

____

Day 28

The Bible tells us that he who wins souls
is wise. Wisdom comes from God. How do
we acquire wisdom? I have often heard
when we exercise our knowledge and by
life experiences we gain wisdom. This may
very well be true however Solomon gained
wisdom simply by asking God. Solomon
was the wisest man to ever live and there
has not been any wiser since his time.
Yes there have been men and women who
are wise - don't misunderstand me on
this. He sought a pearl directly from the
source and the source became his
resource for what he desired. Seek ye first
the kingdom of God and his righteousness
and all these things will be added.
Wisdom was the desire of Solomon's heart
and he was granted that desire. We all
have asked God for some things and those
things have not happened? Did we pray in
faith? I did. However, I also began to
realize that some of the things I prayed for
probably were not what I needed and I
even was not ready for those things. So
how did my prayer change? I prayed
God's will for my life and as long as it has
aligned with His will those prayers will be
answered. Does it mean I won't get the
other things I have prayed for? I'm not
sure, yet I am certain that as long as I
pray in faith (believing that what I ask for

is what God has for me) I will receive those things.

When we allow the Holy Spirit to guide our prayers and acts to glorify God that will also allow our faith to grow. I've often spoken about my new vehicle and how I had to pray and listen when God directed me to the dealership and the salesperson. I've told people this and others have said okay maybe I'll try that and they have, which has ultimately strengthened their relationship with God. Even in this example, I wasn't bragging about me, I was bragging (glorifying) God.

Acts 11:24 "For he was a good man, full of the Holy Spirit and of faith. And a great many people were added to the Lord"

Reflect on times when you listened to God and things worked out and people gained a testimony from your testimony. What are some of those?

____

____

____

____

____

____

____

____

Day 29

I know many pastors who operate in the prophetic anointing of their ministry. I have seen prophesies manifest in others' lives and even in my life. There was a time I had gone through a season of my life: what I had done was wrong and I thought and felt God was mad at me and wouldn't forgive me what had happened. I was walking in shame because I wanted to tell my side of the story yet there was no one who would listen. The other person's side was told and taken as facts. Other people attached to this matter were going around trying to make me be the "bad person" yet all I can say is BUT GOD! I was working as a police officer and went to visit a church on a Sunday morning during my down time and the pastor recognized me called me into the sanctuary and spoke words of life to me. I recall those words even unto this day and this was many years ago. He said "I don't know what God is talking about yet He told me to tell you, you are forgiven". He went on to say "all that was done was a test and you can move on from this point".

I was able to receive this. Not only because I had talked to God about this matter but because I knew this pastor had a defined relationship with God. He was unaware of what happened. I knew it had to be God speaking through him. What I was looking for from man God showed me it wasn't coming from man but from Him. Our faith ignites and fuels our gifts. The more we use our gifts the more that much more refined they become which can ultimately fuel our faith. We see that God is doing what he said he would and can do.

Romans 12:6 "Having then gifts differing according to the grace that is given to us, let us use them: if prophecy, let us prophesy in proportion to our faith".

How can your faith help your gifts become a greater benefit to the body of Christ and glorify God?

____

____

____

____

____

____

____

____

Day 30

As we journey through life we tend to sometimes allow pride to overtake us. It is one thing to have pride it is another to be secure in who you are and your capabilities. I have heard and sometime use a cliché "that that I know I know, I know" simply meaning what I know, no one can take that away from me. There are times I will second guess myself, especially on standardize exams, I despise those things however, I am learning not to second guess myself but believe what I know I do know and not think I am better than anyone else.

In my life I have been adamant that God is God and there is nothing anyone can tell me differently. I often say I would rather live my life believing there is a God and find out there isn't versus living my life as if there is no God and find out there is. I will not force my beliefs on people I will brag about my God. I will tell others about the amazing things He has done in my life and through my life without presenting myself as lofty or better than them because I am not better than anyone. Will you do the same? Will you tell people about the wonderful things He has done for you? Will you brag about him? Today our political climate is one where people need to have faith in God so they know he is still in control and he holds our future in his hands? We can stand on our faith knowing that God has the final say. We have to continue to believe that even if we do not agree with whoever is at 1600 Pennsylvania Avenue we still know a God who has all power and authority and can change everything in the blink of an eye. Don't allow your faith to place you in a lofty position yet allow your faith to place you in a secure position. Your faith has brought you through some muddy issues and it will continue to as long as you stand with who holds your hand and walks with you. Some may not understand or may not have grown as you. Intercede for them and continue to stand.

II Corinthians 1:24 "Not that we have dominion over your faith, but are fellow workers for your joy; for by faith you stand".

Share your experiences of how faith has helped you with one person for the next 7 days. Write down how it helped you and them.

____

____

____

____

____

____

____

NOTES/REFLECTIONS

NOTES/REFLECTIONS

NOTES/REFLECTIONS